Daily Life in Ancient Egypt

by Nicole Walker

illustrated by Wayne Hovis

Harcourt
SCHOOL PUBLISHERS

Copyright © by Harcourt, Inc.

All rights reserved. No part of this publication may be reproduced or transmitted in any form or by any means, electronic or mechanical, including photocopy, recording, or any information storage and retrieval system, without permission in writing from the publisher.

Requests for permission to make copies of any part of the work should be addressed to School Permissions and Copyrights, Harcourt, Inc., 6277 Sea Harbor Drive, Orlando, Florida 32887-6777. Fax: 407-345-2418.

HARCOURT and the Harcourt Logo are trademarks of Harcourt, Inc., registered in the United States of America and/or other jurisdictions.

Printed in China

ISBN 10: 0-15-351703-4
ISBN 13: 978-0-15-351703-7

Ordering Options
ISBN 10: 0-15-351216-4 (Grade 6 Advanced Collection)
ISBN 13: 978-0-15-351216-2 (Grade 6 Advanced Collection)
ISBN 10: 0-15-358186-7 (package of 5)
ISBN 13: 978-0-15-358186-1 (package of 5)

If you have received these materials as examination copies free of charge, Harcourt School Publishers retains title to the materials and they may not be resold. Resale of examination copies is strictly prohibited and is illegal.

Possession of this publication in print format does not entitle users to convert this publication, or any portion of it, into electronic format.

4 5 6 7 8 9 10   0940   12 11 10 09

What do you think of when you imagine ancient Egypt? Do you think of powerful pharaohs and queens like Cleopatra? Perhaps you think of tombs full of mummies, like in the movies? What about the magnificent pyramids and the desert? What about the rest? What was ancient Egypt really like?

The Nile

Any true description of ancient Egypt should probably begin with the river Nile, located in northern Africa. The word *Nile* comes from the word *Neilos*, a Greek name meaning river valley. Another Greek name for the Nile was *Aigyptos*, which itself is the source of the name *Egypt*. The Nile runs through one of the driest deserts in the world, called the Red Lands by the ancient Egyptians. The Red Lands provided the Egyptians with gold and other metals but was an impossible place for humans and most animals to live. However, where the Nile ran through this desert, it created an area of fertile, crop-friendly soil that became Egypt. Egyptians called their country "The Black Land" because the dirt was black with mineral deposits left by the Nile's annual floods.

The river brought life wherever it went. Cheetahs and antelope drank from it during the day, and jackals and hyenas crept down to its banks at night. Crocodiles basked in the shallows, and hippos overturned the boats of unfortunate fishers. Children chased frogs while exotic birds wheeled overhead.

The Nile was—and still is, to some extent—the source of life for all Egyptians. In fact, the Greeks called Egypt "the gift of the Nile" because without the river, Egypt wouldn't have existed. In ancient times, the Nile overflowed its banks once a year, flooding the valley with moisture and nutrients that promoted crop growth. Egyptians abandoned their homes when this happened, returning after the floods to plant their crops. The soil the waters left behind was so moist and fertile that Egyptians barely needed to water the plants until harvest time.

The Nile influenced life in Egypt to such an extent that Egyptians divided their year into three seasons based on

the Nile's flooding pattern: the inundation, (when the river flooded); the growing period; and the drought (when the waters receded, and there was no rain).

During the inundation, there wasn't much for farmers to do. The pharaoh often recruited them to work on building projects during this season. Those who didn't hire themselves out had more time to spend with their families, playing games or sports, or fishing along the Nile. After the flood, farmers rushed back to their homes—or what was left of them. Because the waters destroyed all markers and everything looked different, Egyptians often had trouble figuring out where their property ended and their neighbors' began. Disputes over land were common.

The Nile wasn't always predictable. Sometimes it flooded so much that the Egyptians couldn't plant their crops. Other times, it didn't flood at all. During years when the inundation was either too much or too little, the Egyptians had little food.

Home Life

As a result, life in ancient Egypt was difficult, and Egyptians didn't live very long. The average woman who was a mother lived only thirty years. The average man lived to be about thirty-five. Because their lives were so short compared to life spans today, Egyptians married and began to have children at a very young age: twelve or thirteen for girls and fourteen or fifteen for boys.

The couple's new home was usually small and cramped. Women cooked meals indoors, lighting fires by rubbing two pieces of wood together. Wood was rare, though, so they had to find other things to burn in the fire. To get away from the smoky indoors, and to cool off, Egyptians slept and ate their evening meals on the roof.

Perhaps because wood was rare, Egyptians had little furniture. Chairs were very rare and were reserved for important people. In fact, the hieroglyphic (picture writing) for "dignitary," or important person, was a drawing of a chair. To sit in a chair, if you didn't deserve such distinction, was considered inappropriate. Most Egyptians sat on the ground.

Bathrooms were separate from the main living area and never contained bathtubs. Egyptians thought it was disgusting to sit in unmoving water. Instead, they poured water over themselves, much like the modern shower. Also, instead of soap, they used a cleansing cream made of oil and special scents.

Pets and Other Animals

Households also included pets like cats, birds, and even baby gazelles. Cats were the favorite. Many Egyptians believed that cats could protect their families from harm. Anyone caught killing a cat was put to death. Royalty also kept cats, though sometimes their cats were of a wilder variety—lions and cheetahs lived in the palace in place of house cats.

Some Egyptians also kept baboons for pets. The Egyptians trained baboons to climb trees and pick sycamore fruits and also to fight crime by tracking down thieves. Baboons can pick up scents just like dogs. Trained baboons played an invaluable role in keeping Egyptian crime down.

Meals

Meals were usually simple and centered around the home. Though Egyptians often entertained guests, they didn't gather at restaurants because there were none in ancient Egypt! Also, most meals were vegetarian, except among the wealthy. When poorer Egyptians did eat meat, they were careful to use every part of the animal.

Before the meal began, the host would bring out a small statue of a mummy and place it where the guests or family members could see it while they ate. This statue urged guests to remember that life was short, and they should therefore enjoy the meal and the company as thoroughly as possible.

Bread was present at almost every meal, especially among the common people. Egyptian bread was nourishing but difficult on the teeth. Sand often made its way into the dough and wore down the teeth of those who consumed it.

There were no forks, so guests ate with their hands. However, people were very particular in how they did so. The right way was to eat with the first three fingers of the right hand. Anything else was considered very rude.

Wealthy people held feasts where they watched entertainers like dancers and acrobats. They kept cool and fresh-smelling at these feasts by wearing a cone of perfumed animal fat on their heads. As the fat melted, it dripped onto their faces, releasing its scent.

Children

The Egyptians loved children and gave them as much freedom as possible. Children did very little other than have the time of their lives. Ancient murals show children swimming in the Nile (keeping an eye out for crocodiles!), playing games with balls, riding piggyback, running races, and playing tug-of-war. Parents gave their children time to play, though children of poorer families had to work, running errands or helping their parents at their workplaces. In the evening, parents told their children stories, some of which have survived to this day. For instance, one version of the story of "Cinderella" may have originated in ancient Egypt.

Women

The ethics governing the rights of women were different in ancient times than they are today in most places. However, Egyptian women had a number of opportunities that others in the ancient world did not have. Although Egyptian women weren't educated, they could bring their husbands to court for ill-treatment. They were not banned from owning property. In fact, they owned a third of the property they shared with their husbands, along with whatever belongings they had before they were married. Also, parents left their possessions to their children in equal shares, regardless of their gender.

Without an education, women couldn't work as scribes (the most learned profession), but they did work outside the home and were expected to earn a third of the family's living. They sold homemade goods in the marketplace like cloth, baskets, and clothes, and they worked as shopkeepers, musicians, mill workers, and boat pilots.

Clothing

Ancient Egypt was very hot! Clothes were used more to shield the wearer from the sun than to keep warm.

Women and men went to elaborate lengths to make themselves attractive. They wore lots of jewelry, most of it made from the gold mined in the surrounding desert. Because it was so hot, and because it was so difficult to keep lice and other pests at bay, both men and women frequently shaved their heads and wore wigs for special occasions. Children, in particular, were shaved bald, though boys often kept a lock of hair tied with string that hung from the top of their heads to their shoulders.

Makeup was also very popular. Women wore elaborate makeup on their cheeks, lips, and eyes every day. Men wore eye makeup on special occasions. At fancy parties, women kept their makeup under their chairs in special boxes. One useful by-product of this eye makeup was that it had antibacterial properties and protected the eyes from infection. This was useful at a time when infections could rapidly become very serious. The eye makeup also lessened glare from the sun, much like the black goop football players smear under their eyes today.

Health and Medicine

Egyptians had an advanced understanding of the human body, partly because they learned a lot in the process of mummifying their dead. Still, they knew nothing about germs and believed illness was caused by imagined evil spirits. People frequently died from diseases that are easily cured today.

Parasites like hookworm and roundworm were common because most people went barefoot and only bathed in the dirty river. Deaths from tooth infections were particularly widespread, as dentists didn't know how to remove rotten teeth. There was a strange remedy that dentists *did* prescribe for rotten teeth: fried mice! The logic behind this cure was peculiar: the more horrible the cure, they believed, the more effective it would be at driving illness out of the body.

13

Archeological Remains

What's left of ancient Egypt today? Quite a bit! For one thing, there are the pyramids, where the ancient pharaohs were buried. Some pyramids date as far back as 450 B.C. Archaeologists have also found stones carved with hieroglyphics (ancient Egyptian picture-writing) that provide us with Egyptian myths and stories.

The dry desert air also preserved a lot of other relics. Archaeologists have found pottery, farming tools, and even ancient toys and dolls. If people could afford it, they would get their bodies preserved after death, in the form of mummies. These mummies and their possessions were placed in a tomb so that the person who died would have these things in the afterlife. In a way, this process was an attempt to extend life. Today Egyptian tombs are like time capsules, preserving possessions for those archaeologists lucky enough to unearth them.

Egyptians loved life. They were fully engaged in the pursuit of happiness, whether that meant giving their children the best childhood possible, spending time with their families, or putting on their fancy outfits and looking their best for parties. They, too, liked to swim and tell their children stories. Just like some of us, they held parties and dreaded doctor visits. Maybe their lives weren't really all that different compared to ours— well, aside from fried mice.

Think Critically

1. Why did the Greeks call Egypt "the gift of the Nile"?

2. How do ancient Egyptian meals compare to your meals today?

3. How did the Nile River influence life in ancient Egypt?

4. How was ancient Egyptian medicine different from modern medicine? How were the two the same?

5. Which detail from the book made the biggest impression on you? Why?

Social Studies

Time Line Make a time line of an ancient Egyptian's life. Choose a gender, and be creative in marking specific events in his or her life. How old was she when she got her first pet? How old was she when she got married? At what age did he start his job? When was he hired to build a pyramid for the pharaoh?

School-Home Connection Select three details from the book to share with your family members. Was this information new to them? Did it surprise them? Why or why not?

Word Count: 1,887